Christmas Rising

How the Prophecies of Christ's Birth Encourage Us

Richard K Dickinson

RDickinsonBooks

ISBN: 979-8-218-00307-4

First Edition

For May Yin, a rare treasure amongst the wives who

have walked the earth.

Contents

Introduction

Christmas Rising is intentionally short and meant to be read in a sitting or two, but it is not superficial. The book ties together the prophecies of Daniel, Isaiah, and Micah as referenced in Matthew and Luke, giving the full scope of the Scriptural narrative of Jesus' birth. These Scriptures reveal details that fit together like a puzzle, painting a composite picture of Jesus' identity and authority. Grasping the reality of Jesus is the foundation of hope, and a concrete hope dispels darkness or despair of any kind.

The book encompasses the beautiful parts of the Christmas narrative (Mary's visitation, angels, shepherds, wise men) as well as the hard parts (Herod's slaughter of Bethlehem's children, the judgement on unbelief in Isaiah). It is user friendly as well as serious, with detailed footnotes. What really happened on Christmas? Let us earnestly study the matter and let the truth of Christmas rise up in our hearts, for rightly understanding Christmas will change our lives – forever.

Chapter 1

Origins in the East

S omewhere around 600 BC there was hysteria throughout the ancient kingdom of Babylon because a decree had been issued that all the magi (wise men) throughout the land were to be executed.[1] King Nebuchadnezzar was a powerful king, perhaps the greatest in the ancient world, and he was greatly perplexed and frightened by a dream. He needed to know what the dream meant and needed that knowledge immediately.

The magi were summoned and asked to interpret, which as wise men was part of their job, but in Nebuchadnezzar's request there was a twist. The wise men would certainly come up with some sort of explanation of the dream, possibly even a range of interpretations for the king to review. I suspect he was afraid of this scenario. He didn't want a range of options; he wanted only the correct inter‐pretation. To guarantee this, he first asked them to describe what he had originally dreamed, then give its meaning – that way he could be sure they knew what they were talking about.

The magi were incredulous at this demand. Their response was that no other king in all the kingdoms of the world had ever demanded such a thing. It was not fair, only the gods could give such an answer! When the magi balked at his command, he deemed them worthless as counselors and decided to execute them all.[2]

Ah, but let's not worry too much over their fate because they would soon be rescued by a very inter‐esting young lad. A bit earlier, Nebuchadnezzar's war machine took captive a teenager and a couple of his friends from the land of Judah. Nebuchadnezzar thought it would be instructive to have them in his court, learning the ways and customs of the Chaldeans.[3] He also wanted to test them against his own counselors, a kind of 'foreign exchange' type exercise. And he was quite surprised at the test results – after rigorous training, the young men were found to be ten times better in all aspects![4]

The young lad, who Nebuchadnezzar named Beltes-hazzar, is most commonly known to the world as Daniel. And Daniel had a gift from God; he could interpret dreams. It does not seem he could always do this; it appears it was something God gave him. Why would God do that?

Well, something happened to Daniel when his hometown was raided by Nebuchadnezzar and he was carried off as a prisoner to Babylon. Instead of being bitter and feeling sorry for himself, he decided to strengthen himself mentally and spiritu-ally. He would keep to the writings of the prophets and patriarchs and not participate in practices that would compromise them – quite a remarkable feat for a young teen! In today's world that would be the equivalent of a son or daughter heading off to college with the determination not to get sucked into the decay of the college scene.

To those who seek the face of God, God rewards, blesses, and encourages. Daniel's initial concern was not to defile himself with the king's food, a rather small thing considering he was a prisoner in a foreign land – but faithfulness to God starts in small things and grows one step at a time, does it not?

Being faithful is not insignificant. God rewards faithfulness by bringing us closer to himself and his purposes. A special relationship is born with him. We become not only his children but also his friends, and he reveals to us what he is doing.[5] The king and the entire world were about to learn their fate – all of which was tied up in Nebuchadnezzar's dream – the meaning of which Daniel was about to explain.

Since Daniel lived amongst the other magi and was considered a member of their organization or society, he too was under the death sentence. As everybody was being rounded up for execution, Daniel inquired as to why the punishment was so severe – what had the magi done to deserve this? When told that the other magi had been unable to tell Nebuchadnezzar his dream, Daniel immediately took the matter in hand. He called the king's secretary to book an audience with the king, explaining that he would tell the dream and explain its meaning.[6] Daniel did not yet know the dream at the time of making the appointment, but he trusted God with his life.

After making the appointment, he turned to his friends and asked them to join him in prayer – that very night, as he was sleeping, God showed Daniel the dream and its meaning.[7] He was immediately and with great haste brought before the king, who asked if it was so: could he really retell the dream and interpret? Daniel's answer is instructive and demonstrates his humility and respect for God:

> No wise men, enchanters, magicians, or astrologers can show to the king the mystery that the king has asked, but there is a God in heaven who reveals mysteries, and he has made known to King Nebuchadnezzar what will be in the latter days. Your dream and the visions of your head as you lay in bed are these: To you, O king, as you lay in bed came thoughts of what would be after this, and he who reveals mysteries made known to you what is to be. But as for me, this mystery has been revealed to me, not because of any wisdom that I have more than all the living, but in order that the interpretation may be made known to the king, and that you may know the thoughts of your mind.[8]

Here is the dream, retold in its entirety:

> You saw, O king, and behold, a great image. This image, mighty and of exceeding brightness, stood before you, and its appearance was frightening. The head of this image was of fine gold, its chest

and arms of silver, its middle and thighs of bronze, its legs of iron, its feet partly of iron and partly of clay. As you looked, a stone was cut out by no human hand, and it struck the image on its feet of iron and clay, and broke them in pieces. Then the iron, the clay, the bronze, the silver, and the gold, all together were broken in pieces, and became like the chaff of the summer threshing floors; and the wind carried them away, so that not a trace of them could be found. But the stone that struck the image became a great mountain and filled the whole earth.

This was the dream. Now we will tell the king its interpretation. You, O king, the king of kings, to whom the God of heaven has given the kingdom, the power, and the might, and the glory, and into whose hand he has given, wherever they dwell, the children of man, the beasts of the field, and the birds of the heavens, making you rule over them all – you are the head of gold. Another kingdom inferior to you shall arise after you, and yet a third kingdom of bronze, which shall rule over all the earth. And there shall be a fourth kingdom, strong as iron, because iron breaks to pieces and shatters all things. And like iron that crushes, it shall break and crush all these. And as you saw the feet and toes, partly of potter's clay and partly of iron, it shall be a divided kingdom, but some of the firmness of iron shall be in it, just as you saw iron mixed with the soft clay. And as the toes of the feet were partly iron and partly clay, so the kingdom shall be partly strong and partly brittle. As you saw the iron mixed with soft clay, so they will mix with one another in marriage, but they will not hold together, just as iron does not mix with clay.

And in the days of those kings the God of heaven will set up a kingdom that shall never be destroyed, nor shall the kingdom be left to another people. It shall break in pieces all these kingdoms and bring them to an end, and it shall stand forever, just as you saw that a stone was cut from a mountain by no human hand, and that it broke in pieces the iron, the bronze, the clay, the silver, and the gold. A great God has made known to the king what shall be after this. The dream is certain, and its interpretation sure.[9]

The purpose of the dream was to grant understanding to Nebuchadnezzar (and all who would listen) as to what would happen in the latter days of human history. The dream begins with an image of a warrior, mighty and of exceeding brightness, fiercely towering over everything else in the land, making small in its shadow the esteemed kingdom of Babylon. This was not good news to Nebuchadnezzar. Would he have to fight it? How would he even attack it, and with what? It was a most horrifying warrior, the likes of which no other king had ever seen, and it had come to him.

It gets worse. This warrior image, who Nebuchadnezzar instantly knew was undefeatable, was itself all of a sudden destroyed before his very eyes! A stone, cut by no human hand, smashed the image into pieces such that the winds blew every piece away. The stone then became a mountain and filled the whole earth. There would be nowhere to run, no escape. His dreaded image is torn to shreds by a stone that fills the earth. 'Good grief! I'm going to lose everything!', he must have thought. 'What is this stone and what am I to do?'

As Daniel explained to the king, the image represented a composite of four kingdoms that would appear on earth, of which Nebuchadnezzar's kingdom was the first and perhaps the greatest (he was the head of gold). In reality, the image is man, in all forms, with all his endeavors to rule the earth. All the great kingdoms of man are seen as one.

Thus, standing forebodingly before Nebuchad-nezzar is what we can call the 'man-king', mighty and of exceeding brightness, which is man's attempt to be ruler as God. History has proven this. In every period man has tried to conquer and rule the earth. The 'man-king' looks unstoppable and undefeatable, until a little stone is cut by no human hand and crushes it.

We are told the stone represents another king, not of earth and not born simply of man (cut by no human hand). The God that Daniel served, the God of Abraham, Isaac, and Jacob, the God of Heaven, will set up his own kingdom. His king will rule over all; there will be no end to his kingdom. The 'man-king' will not prevail and will not achieve his desire to completely rule the earth. He will be destroyed and swept aside by the earth's rightful ruler. This is significant, because if all of our treasure is from the realm of the 'man-king' and not from the God of Heaven, what will happen to us? Like Nebuchadnez-zar's concern, will we lose everything?

Some questions arise here. Why does the stone destroy all the other kingdoms? Does it not like to share with the other children? Or could it be that the earthly man-king and its citizenry, laws, morals, decrees, and accomplishments are incompatible with the heavenly kingdom? And how can this new kingdom continue forever and its king reign for thousands and thousands of years without ever ending, unless the king overcomes death?

These thoughts lead us to conclude that the coming king is, indeed, a very special king. The stone cut by no human hand must represent someone who is not only human, but also more than human – a divine king. The magi and Nebuchadnezzar learn that the earth will someday have a divine king!

Do you want to see a reflection of what this divine king looks like compared to Nebuchadnezzar's image? Try this description of Jesus Christ in Revelation:

> Then I turned to see the voice that was speaking to me, and on turning I saw seven golden lampstands, and in the midst of the lampstands one like a son of man, clothed with a long robe and with a golden sash around his chest. The hairs of his head were white, like white wool, like snow. His eyes were like a flame of fire, his feet were like burnished bronze, refined in a furnace, and his voice was like the roar of many waters. In his right hand he held seven stars, from his mouth came a sharp two-edged sword, and his face was

like the sun shining in full strength. When I saw him, I fell at his feet as though dead. But he laid his right hand on me, saying, "Fear not, I am the first and the last, and the living one. I died, and behold I am alive forevermore, and I have the keys of Death and Hades.[10]

Nebuchadnezzar's image did not outshine the sun, it did not have the stars of destiny in its hand, or a voice like roaring water (it actually did not even speak). It was not clothed in white i.e., pure and holy, with piercing eyes like fire able to see into the souls of men. No, Nebuchadnezzar's image was only man's attempt to be God, standing on earth; not the real king who stands in Heaven holding the keys of Death and Hell.

Not only will the stone bring an end to the kingdoms of man; it will also bring an end to death and destruction, sorrow and pain, suffering and darkness. There should be great hope associated with the coming of this stone. There should also be a note of extreme caution, for everything outside of the God of Heaven's kingdom will be destroyed and cast away – the stakes couldn't be higher.

Nebuchadnezzar was overwhelmed with what God had revealed to Daniel and rewarded him with an exalted position in his kingdom and placed him as head over the magi whose lives had been spared.[11]

And, most importantly, a window of understanding into the future and hope of man had been opened, for the world was about to receive a very different kind of king.

Chapter 2

The Magi and Their Journey to Worship

S omeone was paying attention. A new star had appeared in the evening sky and word probably circulated quickly among the magi. They gazed; they researched; they verified its existence; they counseled with one another. What was certain to them was the fact that the star was new to the night sky, and therefore hugely significant. But significant how? We don't know how long it took, but they figured it out.

Here's what we know: like other ancient cultures, the magi would have passed on their history by oral and written tradition. Some five hundred years earlier, their ancestors almost faced extinction under Nebuchadnezzar but were saved by Daniel's God. From that encounter they knew that a new kingdom would arise, a heavenly one, which would replace all other kingdoms as signified by a little stone, cut by no human hand, that would become a mountain and fill the whole earth. The same God of Heaven who would cut the stone must be the same God who hung the new star. Hence, the stone had been cut! The King had arrived, and they wanted to honor him.

Other people, perhaps neighbors or maybe even family members, most likely thought they were delusional; possibly some even mocked them and their theories. It's always that way in this world. Remember, Noah spent one hundred years building an ark to prepare for a great flood, and they laughed at him. Up until then, the earth had been watered only by a mist, not rain,[1] so how could there be a flood? Then one day the doors of the ark were shut and the rains came.

Matthew presents it this way:

> Now after Jesus was born in Bethlehem of Judea in the days of Herod the king, behold, wise men [magi] from the east came to Jerusalem, saying, "Where is he who has been born king of the Jews? For we saw his star when it rose and have come to worship him".[2]

The purpose of the visit? To worship this new king. What a thrill it must have been. Five centuries had elapsed, yet now the time had come. They would soon see him with their own eyes. They would kneel before the stone that would one day fill the whole earth!

The magi came to Jerusalem because that was the ancient capital of Israel where the temple was located, so it was the logical place to look. Except Israel now had a different king, Herod, who ruled under Roman authority. Israel had been unfaithful and the Jews had lost their independence – just as their prophets had warned.

Jerusalem was not happy with this news about the birth of a new king, not happy at all:

> When Herod the king heard this, he was troubled, and all Jerusalem with him.[3]

Troubled? Jerusalem with its people, priests, and rulers did not wish to make room for this new king. It was that simple. They had a well-oiled religious/political machine and enough rules and regulations to control and profit off the masses. A new king meant new leadership, rule change, perhaps even some inquiry into ongoing practices or audits of the books? This was not good news to Jerusalem.

Logic had brought the magi to Jerusalem and to King Herod, but not to the king they were seeking. It would be through Scripture that his whereabouts would be revealed:

> Assembling all the chief priests and scribes of the people, he [Herod] inquired of them where the Christ was to be born. They told him, "In Bethlehem of Judea, for so it is written by the prophet: 'And you, O Bethlehem, in the land of Judah, are by no means least among the rulers of Judah; for from you shall come a ruler who will shepherd my people Israel.'"[4]

A great deal of confusion in life can be resolved by understanding what we are observing here. The star told the magi the King had been born, but it was Scripture that told them where to find him. Although the universe displays the glory of God,[5] it is only Scripture that explains Jesus Christ, his nature, and his work. Centuries earlier, God revealed through the prophet Micah that his son would be born in Bethlehem, and God did not let the magi bypass this encounter with Scripture.

We are not going to be allowed to bypass Scripture either on our journey to understand life. The Bible is really that important.[6] What is written, is written. The King would be found in Bethlehem and nowhere else. This makes life so much simpler. If who we are trusting to guide us was not born in Bethlehem, our savior is an imposter.

> Then Herod summoned the wise men secretly and ascertained from them what time the star had appeared. And he sent them to Bethlehem, saying, "Go and search diligently for the child, and when you have found him, bring me word, that I too may come and worship him."
>
> After listening to the king, they went on their way. And behold, the star that they had seen when it rose went before them until it came to rest over the place where the child was. When they saw the star, they rejoiced exceedingly with great joy. And going into the house, they saw the child with Mary his mother, and they fell down and worshiped him. Then, opening their treasures, they offered him gifts, gold and frankincense and myrrh.
>
> And being warned in a dream not to return to Herod, they departed to their own country by another way.[7]

Herod was crafty. The news of the Jewish King (also referred to as the Messiah or the Christ) having been born was deeply threatening. So before the magi left for Bethlehem, he set up a secret meeting with them and manufactured a countenance of fake devotion, all so that he could ascertain the age of the child because he was planning on killing him. The magi were not immediately aware of this, but God made it known later on through a dream.

As the magi obeyed Scripture and turned towards Bethlehem, the star again appeared, shining directly over Christ's location. Seeing the star again was enormously encouraging and caused great joy. They were correct in their interpretation of events – the stone had been cut – the King was born! Their journey would soon be complete.

Coming before the young child, Jesus Christ, they offered gifts and bowed to the ground. Finding Christ was the desire of their soul and they had found him. All that their forefathers had written about had finally come to pass. Daniel's God, who had saved their ancestors from Nebuchadnezzar's wrath, had now given them a star and then a Scripture to lead them to his son. I am sure they told Mary and all gathered of their quest, the star, their ancestry, their journey. After presenting what appears to be highly significant and royal gifts, they departed, bypassing Herod, for God had warned them about Herod in a dream.

By their homage, they were accepting Christ's reign over them. On the day of judgement, when the books containing all our deeds are opened, we shall see these very magi standing in the Kingdom of God.

We may not see King Herod standing with them, however. He was furious that the magi did not return and report in; and Joseph, being warned in a dream, took the child and his mother and fled:

> Now when they had departed, behold, an angel of the Lord appeared to Joseph in a dream and said, "Rise, take the child and his mother, and flee to Egypt, and remain there until I tell you, for Herod is about to search for the child, to destroy him." And he rose and took the child and his mother by night and departed to Egypt and remained there until the death of Herod...
>
> Then Herod, when he saw that he had been tricked by the wise men [magi], became furious, and he sent and killed all the male children in Bethlehem and in all that region who were two years old or under, according to the time that he had ascertained from the wise men. Then was fulfilled what was spoken by the prophet Jeremiah:

> A voice was heard in Ramah, weeping and loud
> lamentation, Rachel weeping for her children; she
> refused to be comforted, because they are no
> more.[8]

Herod slaughtered all the young male children in Bethlehem and the general region who were two years or younger. This was not only evil; it was by the hand of Satan.[9] There is vehement hatred of Christ throughout the world, for to worship Jesus Christ is against the 'man-king' and all his followers who demand all power for themselves and detest even the thought of God.

> If the world hates you, know that it has hated me
> before it hated you. If you were of the world, the
> world would love you as its own; but because you
> are not of the world, but I chose you out of the
> world, therefore the world hates you.[10]

> Whoever hates me hates my Father also. If I had
> not done among them the works that no one else
> did, they would not be guilty of sin, but now they
> have seen and hated both me and my Father. But
> the word that is written in their Law must be
> fulfilled: They hated me without a cause.[11]

This is the first picture of Christmas that Scripture conveys, in that Matthew is the first Gospel listed in the New Testament. It speaks to the future of all earthly kingdoms which will perish, of a heavenly kingdom without end, and of a King, the Lord Jesus Christ, who rules over death and hell. He will eventually make dust of all the man-king's endeavors and fill the earth with his glory.

Hidden in the magi's journey lies a wonderful truth. It reveals to us in the simplest form the meaning of life: to seek, find, and worship the King is the most important task we can ever accomplish in our lifetime.

Be patient and guard your heart. Some may think you're weird.

Chapter 3

The Prophets and the Coming King

After God destroyed the earth in the Great Flood,[1] only Noah's family was left alive, and one of his three sons, Shem, would give rise to a very famous descendant, Abraham, who in turn would give rise to a very special king, as follows: Abraham begot Isaac, who begot Jacob, who had twelve sons who became the twelve tribes of Israel. One of the tribes, Judah, was singled out to be given dominion. This promise of dominion was given to Judah's most famous king, King David,[2] and it stated that from his lineage would come a king who would sit on David's throne and rule forever, his dominion never being relinquished to another. [3]

Through a series of historical events and prophecies, mostly involving the kings of Israel versus the kings of Syria, Assyria, and Babylon, this coming king who would sit on David's throne was further defined and explained to the world.

Thus, in the middle of the eighth century BC, we find this interesting happening: three kings were having difficulty dividing up and sharing their toys. Ahaz was king of Judah, Pekiah was king of Israel, and Rezin was king of Syria.[4] Rezin and Pekiah wanted Judah for themselves, so Ahaz was distraught; he and his people were actually shaking like branches waving in the wind.[5]

The prophet Isaiah came along and told Ahaz that if he trusted God, he would be delivered from their evil scheme:

> It shall not stand, and it shall not come to pass...
> If you are not firm in faith, you will not be firm at all.[6]

One thing about constant practice for the Olympics is muscle memory. Your body and mind kind of automatically do what you have trained them to do in the midst of tension and stress. The same is true with faith, which becomes stronger and bolder as we trust God in the midst of our personal difficulties. However, Ahaz never bothered to do any of this 'faith' type homework, so he had no confidence in God.

Very well. Isaiah then tells Ahaz to ask a sign from God. Ahaz responds with false humility and says he would not tempt God with such a thing, how dare he suggest it!

Isaiah, at this point exasperated with the king, then says God himself will give you a sign:

> Hear then, O house of David! Is it too little for you to weary men, that you weary my God also? Therefore the Lord himself will give you a sign. Behold, the virgin shall conceive and bear a son, and shall call his name Immanuel.[7]

This prophecy was to strengthen Ahaz by a simple comparison: God is going to cause a virgin to conceive and bear a son who will be called 'Immanuel' or 'God with Us.' Do you think that will be hard for him to do, Ahaz? He can (and will) by his power. So likewise, do you think it is hard for God to solve the problem of your greedy neighbors? That was the implication.

Very similar was Jesus' answer to the Pharisees who condemned him for telling the man who was paralyzed that his sins were forgiven: "Which is easier, to say your sins are forgiven or to say rise and walk?" Whereby Jesus healed the paralytic and he walked away.[8]

Outside of God's power, the thought of a virgin birth is impossible, maybe even preposterous. Really? Didn't we just learn that God hung a star in the night sky for the magi, who were not even Abraham's offspring. Might he not give a little more detail to the descendants of Abraham? The magi were not prophets, but Israel had many of them, and Isaiah was one of the greatest.

Far from being absurd, Isaiah's prophecy furnished the world with more detail on how God would bring forth his ruler to the earth. The future king, Immanuel (God with Us), the stone cut by no human hand, would be born amongst his people through a virgin. Great news! But the warning still stands – if they trusted God's word they would be established, if not, they would fall.

Unfortunately, Ahaz did not believe or trust God to help him with his greedy neighbors and instead sought help from the king of Assyria, which started a domino effect of foreign dominance in the land. Isaiah had warned them; now his people would eventually be subjected to horrible invasions: first by Assyria[9] and then Babylon.

In turmoil and great stress, however, there is always hope. So, Isaiah challenged his people to stop assessing life by their own limited perceptions and by what false prophets were telling them and to start believing and trusting God:

> Do not call conspiracy all that this people calls conspiracy, and do not fear what they fear, nor be in dread. But the LORD of hosts, him you shall honor as holy. Let him be your fear, and let him be your dread.[10]

> And when they say to you, "Inquire of the mediums and the necromancers who chirp and mutter," should not a people inquire of their God? Should they inquire of the dead on behalf of the living?[11]

The Assyrian invasion, which conquered northern Israel in 722 BC, and the Babylonian invasion, which conquered southern Israel (Judah and Jerusalem) in 586 BC, must have looked to the world like the prophecy of a king sitting on David's throne and ruling forever had collapsed. True, Israel would be conquered, her temple burned, her citizens captured or killed. It would be a time of darkness, very little sunlight would pierce through. Ah, but in the darkest times God's hand can move in the most powerful ways, as Isaiah explains in his second prophecy regarding the coming king:

> The people who walked in darkness
> have seen a great light;
> those who dwelt in a land of deep
> darkness, on them has light shone.

> You have multiplied the nation;
> you have increased its joy;
> they rejoice before you
> as with joy at the harvest...

> For to us a child is born,
> to us a son is given; and the government
> shall be upon his shoulder,
> and his name shall be called
> Wonderful Counselor, Mighty God,
> Everlasting Father, Prince of Peace.

> Of the increase of his government
> and of peace there will be no end,
> on the throne of David and over his king-
> dom, to establish it and to uphold it

with justice and with righteousness
from this time forth and forevermore.

The zeal of the LORD of hosts will do
this.[12]

People walking and dwelling in darkness would at
least mean no one knows what they are doing or
where they are going. You can't see or find your way,
physically or morally. There would be no brightness
or hope. You are abandoned, or left fending for
yourself with no true friend. Whichever way you
walk, you trip. Whoever you talk to has no real
answers or solutions or power to implement a way
forward. Without visibility you can't distinguish
friends from enemies, and there would be no relief
from difficult circumstances. Only light can solve
darkness, but what kind of light is meant here?

To begin with, we must believe God and his word –
this is the beginning of gaining light. Isaiah told his
people that if they believed the prophecy that
through the power of God the virgin would
conceive and bear Immanuel (God with us) they
would be established; if not, they would not stand.
The reason for this is simple: believing the
prophecy of Isaiah regarding the virgin birth of
Immanuel was believing God, and if they believed

God, they would be established. This would yield
hope, which is the antithesis of darkness. Thus with
the foreign invasions and overthrow of Israel came
Isaiah's word of hope: people walking in darkness
will see a great light.

More particularly, the light spoken of is connected
with the giving of the child, the child that will
himself be the Son of God, who will sit on David's
throne. There will be no end to his kingdom, and
the government of life will be on his shoulders. He
shall carry within his person the character of
Wonderful Counselor, Mighty God, Everlasting
Father, Prince of Peace. The light spoken of is, ultimately, a person! No matter what the darkness
consists of, the Son of God will be our light. He will
personally lead us and direct us, even if we are
walking through the valley of the shadow of death.[13]

> Again Jesus spoke to them, saying, "I am the light
> of the world. Whoever follows me will not walk in
> darkness, but will have the light of life."[14]

> In him [Jesus] was life, and the life was the light
> of men. The light shines in the darkness, and the
> darkness has not overcome it.[15]

> Long ago, at many times and in many ways, God
> spoke to our fathers by the prophets, but in these

last days he has spoken to us by his Son, whom he appointed the heir of all things, through whom also he created the world. He is the radiance of the glory of God and the exact imprint of his nature, and he upholds the universe by the word of his power...[16]

To the magi God showed a future kingdom that would fill the whole earth, a king represented by a stone, cut by no human hand. To the descendants of Abraham God showed that the king to come will be his own Son, God himself in the flesh, the very creator of the heavens and the earth.[17] He will be born of a virgin and sit on David's throne and rule forever.

If we believe this, he will also be our Prince of Peace, our Counselor, our Mighty God. All of this will come about and be accomplished by the power of God. Those who believe, on them, light will shine. This is what Isaiah told the children of Abraham and the nation of Israel: that in the midst of darkness the Son would come, and the government of life would be on his shoulder. He will rule forever and be the light of life.

> How precious is your steadfast love, O God! The children of mankind take refuge in the shadow of

your wings. They feast on the abundance of your house, and you give them drink from the river of your delights. For with you is the fountain of life; in your light do we see light.[18]

Chapter 4

The Angel Gabriel's Announcement to Mary

Mary, a teenager, appears to be having a normal day. Then, her normal day changed forever. The angel Gabriel had come to explain to her that the prophecy of Isaiah about the virgin birth, some seven centuries earlier, was her prophecy; she was the virgin that would conceive:

> In the sixth month the angel Gabriel was sent from God to a city of Galilee named Nazareth, to a virgin betrothed to a man whose name was Joseph, of the house of David. And the virgin's name was Mary. And he came to her and said, "Greetings, O favored one, the Lord is with you!" But she was greatly troubled at the saying, and tried to discern what sort of greeting this might

be. And the angel said to her, "Do not be afraid, Mary, for you have found favor with God. And behold, you will conceive in your womb and bear a son, and you shall call his name Jesus. He will be great and will be called the Son of the Most High. And the Lord God will give to him the throne of his father David, and he will reign over the house of Jacob forever, and of his kingdom there will be no end."[1]

Gabriel's sudden appearance startled and frightened Mary, so he reassured her. She believed in the God of Abraham and all that the prophets had written. She had found favor with God! Mary had simply been living faithfully before God, going about each day as it unfolded.[2] And God was faithfully going about his plan, for the time had come for his son to enter human history.

Mary's faithfulness had been noticed by God; she had found favor in his eyes. That seems hugely significant. We might do well to ask if such a concept rests amongst our belongings. Is it an integral part of our travel gear; do we rely upon it when planing our future? Which is the more common approach: 'Hey, Rachel, do you think your science teacher will recommend you for the RIT scholarship?' or, 'Hey, Rachel, remember that if you please God he will open the necessary doors – the right doors – that are best for you.[3] Don't worry about your project; you did the best you could. We're proud of you!'

The importance of God's favor is evident with Mary. When she walked out of her house that day she had no idea she would be chosen to be the virgin Isaiah spoke of. Likewise, we have no idea what today's faithfulness to God will mean when tomorrow dawns.

This Scriptural passage says Gabriel was sent by God to Mary. He had no trouble finding her – no Google search, no 'Whitepages' lookup. That's reassuring. God knows all locations of all persons. In the Book of Psalms we read, "God is our refuge and strength, a very present help in trouble."[4] He certainly knows where we are if he is to know if we are in trouble! We are never lost. He is always near.[5]

Notice also how specifically Gabriel described Mary's child: he will be the Son of the Most High. He will sit on David's throne and reign forever, his kingdom never, ever, coming to an end. And he will be called Jesus.

Jesus, or at least his name, is well known in most parts of the world today, but he is not well defined.

Almost always he is discussed in the past tense: Jesus was a good teacher, Jesus was a religious leader, Jesus showed us a good example of how to live (Hollywood refers to Jesus a bit differently). But the angel Gabriel said much more: he will be the Son of the Most High and will reign forever. Now then, if you are reigning forever, you can't be in the past tense. Jesus *is* the Lord, ruling over all, currently.[6]

In response to the Angel's announcement, Mary pointed out a technical difficulty. She was not yet married and therefore still a virgin:

> And Mary said to the angel, "How will this be, since I am a virgin?" And the angel answered her, "The Holy Spirit will come upon you, and the power of the Most High will overshadow you; therefore the child to be born will be called holy —the Son of God. And behold, your relative Elizabeth in her old age has also conceived a son, and this is the sixth month with her who was called barren. For nothing will be impossible with God." And Mary said, "Behold, I am the servant of the Lord; let it be to me according to your word." And the angel departed from her.[7]

The virgin birth will be by the power of God through the Holy Spirit and the child will be called holy – the Son of God. How in the world could such a person arise simply from the human race and be called the son of the Most High, as well as live forever with all the power in the universe?

This child is more than just human – he is human and divine. No mere person could ever be described as this child has been. We are weak and imperfect, that is why all human saviors, rulers, or whatever you wish to call them can never rescue the human race. What the world needs is someone greater than the world, greater than death, to defeat the world and death. Being born of a virgin is an absolute necessity, not a fairy tale. The power of God through the Holy Spirit joins the eternal Son of God to Mary's flesh, creating a person who is fully human and fully divine.

Just because we might not grasp how God could cause a virgin to conceive and bear 'the Son of God', we should not conclude that he can't do it. The magi's star and the virgin birth are simply part of God's wondrous plan that we have the privilege of watching unfold. Let's not restrict God so much in our minds. He is who he is:

> For by him [Jesus] all things were created, in heaven and on earth, visible and invisible, whether thrones or dominions or rulers or author-

ities – all things were created through him and for him. And he is before all things, and in him all things hold together.[8]

In the end, the issue is settled in Mary's mind. If this is what God wants, he will bring it about. She simply went on her way, letting the plan unfold. "Let it be to me according to your word," she told the angel.

Later, filled with awe and wonderment, Mary burst forth in a song of praise to the Lord. She was a very humble and grateful recipient of God's unfolding grace and she loved him and told him so:

My soul magnifies the Lord,

and my spirit rejoices in God my Savior...

for he who is mighty has done great things for me...

And his mercy is for those who fear him

from generation to generation...

he has scattered the proud in the thoughts of their hearts...

and exalted those of humble estate...

He has helped his servant Israel,

in remembrance of his mercy,

as he spoke to our fathers,

to Abraham and to his offspring forever[9]

Her song of praise, referred to as the Magnificat, has a very personal understanding of how God has touched her life. It also contains an understanding of God's prophetic word being realized in his promises to Abraham and his offspring. This is startling. Mary sees the hand of God at work through two thousand years of prophecy,[10] and we want to give up because we didn't perceive God helping us yesterday!

When the angel departed, Mary went and visited her relative Elizabeth for several months before returning to Nazareth. Her fiancé, Joseph, was going to divorce her quietly because of her unwed pregnancy, but God showed him in a dream that it was all true – as a virgin, Mary would bring forth the Messiah.[11]

Another technical difficulty now surfaces, and this one is not noticed by Mary. As she remains in

Nazareth, she is somewhat off course, geographi-
cally speaking. She is pregnant and near term, but
the promised Messiah, as we learned through Scripture, is to be born in Bethlehem.[12] And Mary
doesn't seem to be making any travel plans!

Quite possibly she has enough on her mind, so
God's sovereign hand quietly moves the pieces into
position:

> In those days a decree went out from Caesar
> Augustus that all the world should be registered.
> This was the first registration when Quirinius was
> governor of Syria. And all went to be registered,
> each to his own town. And Joseph also went up
> from Galilee, from the town of Nazareth, to
> Judea, to the city of David, which is called Bethle-
> hem, because he was of the house and lineage of
> David, to be registered with Mary, his betrothed,
> who was with child.[13]

You may look at this any way you wish, but do
justice to God's sovereignty in your mind. Mary is in
Nazareth but is supposed to be in Bethlehem for
the child's birth. It may appear implausible to us,
but God put it into the mind of the Roman king,
Caesar Augustus, to take a census which forced
Joseph and Mary to go to Bethlehem. The most

powerful emperor at the time makes a decree which ensures that the birth of the Son of God will fulfill Scripture by taking place in the correct city!

God moved the pieces according to his plan, and he will bring about what is needed in our lives as well. He is the Architect of the Universe; nothing is impossible for him. Life may sometimes appear to hide his hand, for there will be times when we feel all alone and discouraged. Paul understood this:

> For now we see in a mirror dimly, but then face to face. Now I know in part; then I shall know fully, even as I have been fully known.[14]

Even in the face of many personal difficulties we should take heart. After seven hundred years of prophecy, God brought forth his Son through a virgin and then had the Roman emperor ensure Mary's timely arrival at Bethlehem. God put his chosen King on David's throne and there was no power or force in the universe that could stop him. He moved all the pieces into position and he will oversee our lives as well. We are a part of his plan. Let us trust him more and worry less:

> For I know the plans I have for you, declares the LORD, plans for welfare and not for evil, to give

you a future and a hope. Then you will call upon me and come and pray to me, and I will hear you. You will seek me and find me, when you seek me with all your heart. I will be found by you, declares the LORD...[15]

Chapter 5

The Birth of Christ

Bethlehem had an alternate name, 'City of David' and became famous by name, when King David became famous by deed. Earlier than David, another important person dwelt there: Ruth, the Moabite, David's great grandmother.[1] This small town, then, was very intimately tied to King David's heritage.

Notwithstanding, an even greater prominence was given it by the prophet Micah: the Ruler of Israel, the Messiah, would be born in Bethlehem.[2] We know that Micah prophesied somewhere around 750 to 680 BC and was a contemporary of Isaiah. This gives Bethlehem greater than seven centuries of prophetic prominence as the birthplace of the coming King.

However, at the time of Mary's visit, the Bethlehemites had failed to do what the magi had
succeeded in doing – the magi kept alive their
unique heritage amongst their descendants, whereas
the Bethlehemites seem to have forgotten theirs.
One wonders if they quit teaching their children the
important truths regarding their heritage, for it is
unfathomable that no one in Bethlehem was willing
to make room for Mary – she had to give birth
amongst the animals:

> And while they [Joseph and Mary] were there
> [Bethlehem], the time came for her to give birth.
> And she gave birth to her firstborn son and
> wrapped him in swaddling cloths and laid him in a
> manger, because there was no place for them in
> the inn.[3]

Had the Bethlehemites been alert they might have
recognized something special about Mary. I might
be mistaken, but it seems to me that this young
woman would be tremendously excited and in great
wonderment about the child she would soon birth.
After all, she had talked with the angel Gabriel face
to face; she was a virgin and yet became pregnant by
God's power, and was told her child would be the
Son of the Most High. How could she not be in
tremendous awe and have the brightest of counte-

nances, noticeable to all! Yet, if a people became dull in heart towards God and asleep to their heritage, the ship could very well sail past them, could it not?

Despite the apathy encountered at Bethlehem, there is a brighter understanding here. God allowed his Son to be born in a stable rather than a palace or castle as an example that he would be a savior accessible to all. No invitations needed, no guards at the gate checking credentials, no turnstiles with desk security watching every move. Jesus' humble birth is a statement to the world that we can come to him; we can approach him. In Jesus' own words:

> Come to me, all who labor and are heavy laden, and I will give you rest. Take my yoke upon you, and learn from me, for I am gentle and lowly in heart, and you will find rest for your souls. For my yoke is easy, and my burden is light.[4]

This truth that Jesus would be a savior accessible to all is further evidenced by the angelic visitation upon a small group of ordinary shepherds. A routine evening, simply caring for their sheep under the night sky, and this happens:

And in the same region there were shepherds out
in the field, keeping watch over their flock by
night. And an angel of the Lord appeared to
them, and the glory of the Lord shone around
them, and they were filled with great fear. And
the angel said to them, "Fear not, for behold, I
bring you good news of great joy that will be for
all the people. For unto you is born this day in the
city of David a Savior, who is Christ the Lord.[5]

Ordinary shepherds saw the glory of the Lord and
the heavenly host of angels! Do you know that this
was the first time common people saw the glory of
God? True, God showed his glory to Moses and the
Israelites on Mt. Sinai during the giving of the Ten
Commandments and the building of the tabernacle
and temple, and various patriarchs and prophets saw
his glory in dreams and visions. But something
much greater is evident here. With the coming of
Christ and his work of atonement, the glory of God
is no longer going to be hidden from ordinary
people, from us who believe in him:

Father, I desire that they also, whom you have
given me, may be with me where I am, to see my
glory that you have given me because you loved
me before the foundation of the world.[6]

When Adam and Eve sinned and rebelled against God, getting banned from the Garden of Eden,[7] paradise was lost to mankind and with it the opportunity of seeing God – God literally used to visit and talk with Adam in the Garden of Eden.[8] Over the years people have written about paradise, tried to establish paradise-like utopias, lived on mountains, lived on islands, meditated, taken drugs, flocked to the Himalayas, etc., but none of these opened a door to a true paradise of any significance. Paradise has been lost and so has seeing the glory of God. But the hiddenness of God's glory will come to an end due to the very child who is called Wonderful Counselor, Almighty God, Prince of Peace. The shepherds saw the glory of heaven and so shall we if we belong to Christ.

If we want to put a value on the importance of seeing God's glory, ponder this: how significant is it for the builder of the house to be able to look at the architectural blueprints? We simply cannot comprehend who we are without understanding who made us, for we were meant to have the glory of God shining out from us.[9] This loss has been incalculable to mankind, although we are completely oblivious to it. Instead of radiating God's glory, we often just plod along occupying ourselves with material things, exercise classes, social clubs or hobbies, our phones,

tweets, texts, and so forth – are you familiar with
the dying grasshopper in Ecclesiastes?

Remember also your Creator in the days of your
youth, before the evil days come and the years
draw near of which you will say, "I have no plea-
sure in them"; before the sun and the light and
the moon and the stars are darkened and the
clouds return after the rain, in the day when the
keepers of the house tremble, and the strong men
are bent, and the grinders cease because they are
few, and those who look through the windows are
dimmed, and the doors on the street are shut—
when the sound of the grinding is low, and one
rises up at the sound of a bird, and all the daugh-
ters of song are brought low— they are afraid also
of what is high, and terrors are in the way; the
almond tree blossoms, the grasshopper drags
itself along, and desire fails, because man is going
to his eternal home, and the mourners go about
the streets— before the silver cord is snapped, or
the golden bowl is broken, or the pitcher is shattered at the fountain, or the wheel broken at the
cistern, and the dust returns to the earth as it was,
and the spirit returns to God who gave it. Vanity
of vanities... all is vanity. [10]

That is certainly not a description of the shepherds after seeing the Glory of God. They were excited beyond measure! Nor will it be of anyone who is touched by Christ. Adam lost paradise, but now something much greater than paradise is here. Good news of great joy, for a Savior, who is Christ the Lord, has been given!

The antithesis to the dying grasshopper is this:

> Then I saw a new heaven and a new earth, for the first heaven and the first earth had passed away, and the sea was no more. And I saw the holy city, new Jerusalem, coming down out of heaven from God, prepared as a bride adorned for her husband. And I heard a loud voice from the throne saying, "Behold, the dwelling place of God is with man. He will dwell with them, and they will be his people, and God himself will be with them as their God. He will wipe away every tear from their eyes, and death shall be no more, neither shall there be mourning, nor crying, nor pain anymore, for the former things have passed away."[11]

No other birth on earth had such a glorious and majestic reception as that of Christ's. Look at all the people who are famous or important, whether religious, political, pop icons, sports, cinema, etc. None had angels singing or opened the heavens at their birth. Only the Son of David, the Son of the Most High, the stone uncut by any human hand, had such an attendance on the day of his birth. And mankind was invited to see him because he was accessible, lying quietly in a stable. Who else is offering us the opportunity of seeing the glory of God?

The shepherds were in awe, but they were also terrified – filled with great fear. Why the fear? An episode with Jesus' disciple, Peter, helps explain the fear. He went fishing with Jesus; fishing was Peter's occupation. He was very comfortable with Jesus in the boat, kind of like pals. 'I got this', Peter must have been thinking, hoping he could show Jesus a thing or two. Then Jesus performed a miracle in a great catch of fish, which changed Peter's perspective. He and Jesus weren't equals or pals – Jesus was great and holy, and Peter felt unclean and cried out, "Depart from me for I am a sinful man".[12]

Mankind usually feels just fine because we compare ourselves to one another, which is not a very high standard on the heavenly scale. But should we be given a glimpse of God's glory and correctly perceive the true identity of Jesus as the Son of the Most High God, then his holiness and majesty reveals to us, as to Peter, that we are unclean and sinful, and we become afraid – and rightfully so.

> And the angel said to them, "Fear not, for behold,
> I bring you good news of great joy that will be for
> all the people. For unto you is born this day in the
> city of David a Savior, who is Christ the Lord."[13]

Fear not, good news, great joy – for us? How can that be! We are broken. We have messed up lives. Our spiritual vision is so cloudy we can't even comprehend that we are made in the Image of God, the highest beings in the entire universe next to God Himself![14] And eventually, we all die,[15] death being the terrible price for disobeying God.[16.] We have every reason to be afraid, or do we?

The above Scripture tells us not to be afraid for there is good news of great joy – a Savior has been given. He will rescue us; he will place God's favor upon us. Instead of condemnation there will be peace and forgiveness. Note, however, that the 'good news' and 'great joy' is only associated with this Savior and nothing else – not good fortune, a spouse, a new home, career advancement, children or grandchildren – wonderful as they may be. Good news of great joy is only associated with this partic- ular person, period. Looking elsewhere will not bring the promised joy or peace or hope. Like the fine print at the bottom of the menu, 'No substitutions allowed'.

After the announcement of the Savior's birth, the shepherds are invited to go see for themselves what God has done. As the invitation is given, very suddenly, the whole night sky erupts with a heavenly host of angels praising and worshipping God:

> And this will be a sign for you: you will find a baby wrapped in swaddling cloths and lying in a manger." And suddenly there was with the angel a multitude of the heavenly host praising God and saying, "Glory to God in the highest, and on earth peace among those with whom he is pleased!"[17]

From God on high, peace is given to those who believe in him – not condemnation, not judgement, but peace – and if peace, then forgiveness. The life of this child will ultimately bring peace between God and those who trust him. Anyone who earnestly seeks after Jesus Christ will find true peace because Jesus is the Savior, and associated with him is good news of great joy.

Stirred in their hearts beyond anything they ever experienced, the shepherds made haste to go to Bethlehem:

When the angels went away from them into heaven, the shepherds said to one another, "Let us go over to Bethlehem and see this thing that has happened, which the Lord has made known to us."

And they went with haste and found Mary and Joseph, and the baby lying in a manger. And when they saw it, they made known the saying that had been told them concerning this child. And all who heard it wondered at what the shepherds told them. But Mary treasured up all these things, pondering them in her heart.

And the shepherds returned, glorifying and praising God for all they had heard and seen, as it had been told them.[18]

I believe it is safe to say that the shepherds' lives were never the same again. When we were first introduced to them they were simply out under the night sky tending sheep. In the last snapshot they are praising and glorifying God for all they had seen and heard. The good news of great joy had overflowed upon them. They were the first to have an audience with the Son of God,[19] the stone cut by no human hand, the Savior of the world, because the Most High God invited them to come and see his son, the Lord Jesus Christ. Is that not awesome –

ordinary shepherds were the first to see the
newborn King! Now then, if ordinary shepherds
were invited, so are we. There is a tremendous
amount of love and welcome being poured out on
behalf of mankind by God the Father to encourage
us to arise, like the shepherds, and come to his Son!

> The Spirit of the Lord is upon me, because he has
> anointed me to proclaim good news to the poor.
> He has sent me to proclaim liberty to the captives
> and recovering of sight to the blind, to set at
> liberty those who are oppressed, to proclaim the
> year of the Lord's favor.[20]

Chapter 6

Christmas

There was a man who had walked across an old field, possibly most of his life. It may help to picture a small, rural, Middle Eastern village with surrounding fields – some for grazing, some for crops, some just lying fallow, possibly even some left unattended out of disinterest. There was nothing extraordinary about any of the fields; he was familiar with them all; they just existed near his home, nothing more. But one day, one field was suddenly different. We don't know why – possibly a rainstorm had eroded part of it, or he stubbed his sandal on an object sticking out of the soil. At any rate, something made him pay attention and take a closer look, and upon doing so, he discovered a treasure.

In 2014, there was a California couple who had a
similar experience. A hill on their property, which
they had walked over many times, all of a sudden
had something sticking out of the soil – an old rusty
can, which upon closer examination contained
coins, gold coins, which ended up being worth over
ten million dollars.

It is the same with the man we have been talking
about. Upon a closer look, he discovered a treasure
so valuable that he sold everything to raise the
money necessary to buy the field:

> The kingdom of heaven is like treasure hidden in
> a field, which a man found and covered up. Then
> in his joy he goes and sells all that he has and buys
> that field.[1]

In this parable, Jesus is understood to be the treasure. The field hides the treasure, until someone
takes a closer look. And Jesus, like the field, looks
like a normal person at first glance – just an ordinary
guy, until one takes a closer look. Hidden in plain
sight, dressed as an ordinary man, walking and
eating and sleeping like everyone else – is the Son of
God, the stone cut by no human hand, the King
who sits on David's throne, mankind's only Savior.
So valuable and so wonderful is he, that he is worth

absolutely anything we must go through to understand and love him.

> The true light, which gives light to everyone, was coming into the world. He was in the world, and the world was made through him, yet the world did not know him. He came to his own, and his own people did not receive him. But to all who did receive him, who believed in his name, he gave the right to become children of God, who were born, not of blood nor of the will of the flesh nor of the will of man, but of God.[2]

This book was written that you might have Christmas. You will need to push past the superficiality of the season to take a closer look at the Scriptures and events that make up the birth of Christ, for they reveal him. He is the treasure, albeit hidden at first glance, but Jesus is there and he is there for you. You are made by him and for him. Talk to him. Give him your heart and your life, and let him fill you with his love and glory.

Merry Christmas.

Notes

1. Origins in the East

1. Daniel 2: 12 Because of this the king was angry and very furious, and commanded that all the wise men of Babylon be destroyed.

2. Daniel 2:2-11 Then the king commanded that the magicians, the enchanters, the sorcerers, and the Chaldeans be summoned to tell the king his dreams. So they came in and stood before the king. And the king said to them, "I had a dream, and my spirit is troubled to know the dream." Then the Chaldeans said to the king in Aramaic, "O king, live forever! Tell your servants the dream, and we will show the interpretation." The king answered and said to the Chaldeans, "The word from me is firm: if you do not make known to me the dream and its interpretation, you shall be torn limb from limb, and your houses shall be laid in ruins. But if you show the dream and its interpretation, you shall receive from me gifts and rewards and great honor. Therefore show me the dream and its interpretation." They answered a second time and said, "Let the king tell his servants the dream, and we will show its interpretation." The king answered and said, "I know with certainty that you are trying to gain time, because you see that the word from me is firm— if you do not make the dream known to me, there is but one sentence for you. You have agreed to speak lying and corrupt words before me till the times change. Therefore tell me the dream, and I shall know that you can show me its interpretation." The Chaldeans answered the king and said, "There is not a man on earth who can meet the king's demand, for no great and powerful king has asked such a thing of any magician or enchanter or Chaldean. The thing that the king asks is difficult, and no one can show it

to the king except the gods, whose dwelling is not with flesh."

3. The names Babylon, Babylonians, Chaldeans are used interchangeably in Daniel

4. Daniel 1: 20 And in every matter of wisdom and understanding about which the king inquired of them, he found them ten times better than all the magicians and enchanters that were in all his kingdom.

5. John 15:15 No longer do I call you servants, for the servant does not know what his master is doing; but I have called you friends, for all that I have heard from my Father I have made known to you.

6. Daniel 2:15-16 He declared to Arioch, the king's captain, "Why is the decree of the king so urgent?" Then Arioch made the matter known to Daniel. And Daniel went in and requested the king to appoint him a time, that he might show the interpretation to the king.

7. Daniel 2: 17-19 Then Daniel went to his house and made the matter known to Hananiah, Mishael, and Azariah, his companions, and told them to seek mercy from the God of heaven concerning this mystery, so that Daniel and his companions might not be destroyed with the rest of the wise men of Babylon. Then the mystery was revealed to Daniel in a vision of the night. Then Daniel blessed the God of heaven.

8. Daniel 2:27-30

9. Daniel 2: 31-45

10. Revelation 1:12-18

11. Daniel 2:46-49 Then King Nebuchadnezzar fell upon his face and paid homage to Daniel, and commanded that an offering and incense be offered up to him. The king answered and said to Daniel, "Truly, your God is God of gods and Lord of kings, and a revealer of mysteries, for you have been able to reveal this mystery." Then the king gave Daniel high honors and many great gifts, and made him ruler over the whole province of Babylon and chief prefect over all the wise men of Babylon. Daniel made a request of the king, and he appointed Shadrach, Meshach, and Abed-

nego over the affairs of the province of Babylon. But Daniel remained at the king's court.

2. The Magi and Their Journey to Worship

1. Genesis 2: 5,6 For the LORD God had not caused it to rain on the land, and there was no man to work the ground, and a mist was going up from the land and was watering the whole face of the ground—

2. Matthew 2:1-2

3. Matthew 2:3

4. Matthew 2: 4-6

5. Romans 1:20 For his invisible attributes, namely, his eternal power and divine nature, have been clearly perceived, ever since the creation of the world, in the things that have been made.

6. If you are new to the Bible, I suggest picking up an easy to read translation (the English Standard Version is quoted in this book), and read Matthew or Luke, followed by John, then Genesis – then keep reading!

7. Matthew 2:7-12

8. Matthew 2:16-18

9. Revelation 12: 1-5 And a great sign appeared in heaven: a woman clothed with the sun, with the moon under her feet, and on her head a crown of twelve stars. She was pregnant and was crying out in birth pains and the agony of giving birth. And another sign appeared in heaven: behold, a great red dragon, with seven heads and ten horns, and on his heads seven diadems. His tail swept down a third of the stars of heaven and cast them to the earth. And the dragon stood before the woman who was about to give birth, so that when she bore her child he might devour it. She gave birth to a male child, one who is to rule all the nations with a rod of iron, but her child was caught up to God and to his throne...

10. John 15: 18,19

11. John 15:23-25

3. The Prophets and the Coming King

1. Genesis 6: 5-8 The LORD saw that the wickedness of man was great in the earth, and that every intention of the thoughts of his heart was only evil continually. And the LORD regretted that he had made man on the earth, and it grieved him to his heart. So the LORD said, "I will blot out man whom I have created from the face of the land, man and animals and creeping things and birds of the heavens, for I am sorry that I have made them." But Noah found favor in the eyes of the LORD.

2. 2 Samuel 7: 28-29 And now, O Lord GOD, you are God, and your words are true, and you have promised this good thing to your servant. Now therefore may it please you to bless the house of your servant, so that it may continue forever before you. For you, O Lord GOD, have spoken, and with your blessing shall the house of your servant be blessed forever.

3. 2 Samuel 7:16 'And your house and your kingdom shall be made sure forever before me. Your throne shall be established forever.'

4. After Solomon, Israel became embroiled in a civil war and was divided- the northern tribes vs. Judah.

5. Isaiah 7:2 When the house of David was told, "Syria is in league with Ephraim," the heart of Ahaz and the heart of his people shook as the trees of the forest shake before the wind.

6. Isaiah 7:7-9 "'It shall not stand, and it shall not come to pass. For the head of Syria is Damascus, and the head of Damascus is Rezin. And within sixty-five years Ephraim will be shattered from being a people. And the head of Ephraim is Samaria, and the head of Samaria is the son of Remaliah. If you are not firm in faith, you will not be firm at all.'"

7. Isaiah 7:13-14

8. Mark 2:8-12 "Why do you question these things in your hearts? Which is easier, to say to the paralytic, 'Your sins are forgiven,' or to say, 'Rise, take up your bed and walk'? But that you may know that the Son of Man has authority on earth to forgive sins"—he said to the paralytic— "I say to you, rise, pick up your bed, and go home." And he rose and immediately picked up his bed and went out before them all, so that they were all amazed and glorified God, saying, "We never saw anything like this!"

9. Isaiah 7: 17 "The LORD will bring upon you and upon your people and upon your father's house such days as have not come since the day that Ephraim departed from Judah—the king of Assyria!"

10. Isaiah 8: 12,13

11. Isaiah 8:19

12. Isaiah 9: 2-7

13. Psalm 23 The LORD is my shepherd; I shall not want. He makes me lie down in green pastures. He leads me beside still waters. He restores my soul. He leads me in paths of righteousness for his name's sake. Even though I walk through the valley of the shadow of death, I will fear no evil, for you are with me; your rod and your staff, they comfort me. You prepare a table before me in the presence of my enemies; you anoint my head with oil; my cup overflows. Surely goodness and mercy shall follow me all the days of my life, and I shall dwell in the house of the LORD forever.

14. John 8:12

15. John 1: 4,5

16. Hebrews 1: 1-3

17. John 1:1-3 In the beginning was the Word, and the Word was with God, and the Word was God. He was in the beginning with God. All things were made through him, and without him was not any thing made that was made.

18. Psalm 36: 7-9

4. The Angel Gabriel's Announcement to Mary

1. Luke 1: 26-33
2. Psalm 121: 8 The LORD will keep your going out and your coming in from this time forth and forevermore.
3. Revelation 3:8 I know your works. Behold, I have set before you an open door, which no one is able to shut. I know that you have but little power, and yet you have kept my word and have not denied my name...
4. Psalm 46:1-3 God is our refuge and strength, a very present help in trouble. Therefore we will not fear though the earth gives way, though the mountains be moved into the heart of the sea, though its waters roar and foam, though the mountains tremble at its swelling.
5. Psalm 139: 7-12 Where shall I go from your Spirit? Or where shall I flee from your presence? If I ascend to heaven, you are there! If I make my bed in Sheol, you are there! If I take the wings of the morning and dwell in the uttermost parts of the sea, even there your hand shall lead me, and your right hand shall hold me. If I say, "Surely the darkness shall cover me, and the light about me be night," even the darkness is not dark to you; the night is bright as the day, for darkness is as light with you.
6. Revelation 1:5 Jesus Christ the faithful witness, the firstborn of the dead, and the ruler of kings on earth.
7. Luke 1: 34-38
8. Colossians 1:15-17
9. Luke 1:46-55 And Mary said, "My soul magnifies the Lord, and my spirit rejoices in God my Savior, for he has looked on the humble estate of his servant. For behold, from now on all generations will call me blessed; for he who is mighty has done great things for me, and holy is his name. And his mercy is for those who fear him from generation to generation. He has shown strength with his arm; he has scattered the proud in the thoughts of their hearts; he has brought down the mighty from their thrones and exalted those of

humble estate; he has filled the hungry with good things, and the rich he has sent away empty. He has helped his servant Israel, in remembrance of his mercy, as he spoke to our fathers, to Abraham and to his offspring forever."

10. Abraham lived circa 2100 BC

11. Matthew 1:19-20 And her husband Joseph, being a just man and unwilling to put her to shame, resolved to divorce her quietly. But as he considered these things, behold, an angel of the Lord appeared to him in a dream, saying, "Joseph, son of David, do not fear to take Mary as your wife, for that which is conceived in her is from the Holy Spirit."

12. Micah 5:2 But you, O Bethlehem Ephrathah, who are too little to be among the clans of Judah, from you shall come forth for me one who is to be ruler in Israel, whose coming forth is from of old, from ancient days.

13. Luke 2:1-5

14. 1Corinthians 13:12

15. Jeremiah 29: 11-14

5. The Birth of Christ

1. David reigned circa 1010-970 BC

2. Micah 5:2 But you, O Bethlehem Ephrathah, who are too little to be among the clans of Judah, from you shall come forth for me one who is to be ruler in Israel, whose coming forth is from of old, from ancient days.

3. Luke 2:6-7

4. Matthew 11: 28-30

5. Luke 2: 8-11

6. John 17:24

7. Genesis 3:23-24 Therefore the LORD God sent him out from the garden of Eden to work the ground from which he was taken. He drove out the man, and at the east of the garden of Eden he placed the cherubim and a flaming sword that turned every way to guard the way to the tree of life.

8. Genesis 3:8 And they heard the sound of the LORD God walking in the garden in the cool of the day, and the man

and his wife hid themselves from the presence of the LORD God among the trees of the garden.

9. 2Corinthians 3:18 And we all, with unveiled face, beholding the glory of the Lord, are being transformed into the same image from one degree of glory to another. For this comes from the Lord who is the Spirit.

10. Ecclesiastes Chapter 12: 1-8

11. Revelation 21:1-4

12. Luke 5:3-9 Getting into one of the boats, which was Simon's, he asked him to put out a little from the land. And he sat down and taught the people from the boat. And when he had finished speaking, he said to Simon, "Put out into the deep and let down your nets for a catch." And Simon answered, "Master, we toiled all night and took nothing! But at your word I will let down the nets." And when they had done this, they enclosed a large number of fish, and their nets were breaking. They signaled to their partners in the other boat to come and help them. And they came and filled both the boats, so that they began to sink. But when Simon Peter saw it, he fell down at Jesus' knees, saying, "Depart from me, for I am a sinful man, O Lord." For he and all who were with him were astonished at the catch of fish that they had taken...

13. Luke 2:10,11

14. Genesis 1:26-27 Then God said, "Let us make man in our image, after our likeness. And let them have dominion over the fish of the sea and over the birds of the heavens and over the livestock and over all the earth and over every creeping thing that creeps on the earth." So God created man in his own image, in the image of God he created him; male and female he created them.

15. Romans 5:12 Therefore, just as sin came into the world through one man, and death through sin, and so death spread to all men because all sinned.

16. Genesis 2:15-17 The LORD God took the man and put him in the garden of Eden to work it and keep it. And the LORD God commanded the man, saying, "You may surely eat of every tree of the garden, but of the tree of the knowl-

edge of good and evil you shall not eat, for in the day that you eat of it you shall surely die."

17. Luke 2:12-14
18. Luke 2: 15-20
19. The shepherds saw Jesus the night he was born; the wise men's quest and journey took about two years before they found him.
20. Luke 4: 18,19

6. Christmas

1. Matthew 13:44
2. John 1:9-13

Acknowledgments

Scripture references are from the English Standard Version (ESV). Cynthia Bezek, a longtime family friend and published author, offered very helpful editorial and content guidance. David Monteath, my friend in Britain, contributed helpful editorial suggestions and expressed much enthusiasm over the book's contents. Dr. David Pao, Academic Dean, Trinity Evangelical Divinity School, graciously gave his time to read my draft; his comments helped me clarify my focus in certain chapters. Dan Larison, pastoral staff, Parkside Church, helped me think about the overall flow of the book. Two longtime family friends helped in proof reading: Randy Welsh, a classmate at Trinity Evangelical Divinity School; and Jenifer Deming, a fellow alum of the Northfield Mount Hermon School (all remaining mistakes are mine!). Dr. John J. Taylor, University of Montana, my thesis advisor, encouraged me to write.

About the Author

After wandering around in the vast, arid wasteland of evolution for most of his academic career (BS, MS), Richard Dickinson finally understood evolution for what it is: a hoax. Sitting at his desk writing his Masters' thesis, he realized that if his experiments were accurate, the results should be repeatable by someone else performing the same experiment, even if they were on the other side of the globe. Then the light switched on. How do you get repeatable results in evolution's system of randomness and chance? It would be impossible. No two identical experiments could ever have the same results in such a system, therefore no experiment could ever be verified. Thus, the universe cannot be some chaotic, random, mindless, directionless progression; rather, it evidences structure, organization, and brilliant planning. Life did not 'happen'; it was created. Someone actually was behind the curtain.

It then took Dickinson a while to understand who was telling the truth about God, as he wandered around another vast, arid wasteland: spiritual enlightenment. After delving into the cultural hub of the mystics, combined with rigorous dietary restrictions and extreme fastings; eventually, and thankfully, Dickinson emerged from his enlightenment prison by coming to believe in Jesus Christ as King and Lord.

Eager to learn more about this Savior who had rescued him, he headed back to grad school to study the Bible (M.Div., Trinity Evangelical Divinity School), and for the past 40 years has spent his life pastoring small churches and working as a microbiologist in the indoor air quality (IAQ) sector.

This book on Christmas has been on Dickinson's heart for more than two decades. It needed to be written; and so, he wrote it.

Also by Richard K Dickinson

Easter and the Garden of Eden: The Fall and Redemption
of Man